THE MEANINGFUL VOLUME OF EXISTENCE

By Julian Hamer

Dedicated to my beautiful wife Ellen

THE MEANINGFUL VOLUME OF EXISTENCE
An Exploration of the Overlooked Intangible Significance
of Phenomena

By Julian Hamer

Contents

Introduction

Introduction

We unwittingly sustain a narrow perspective towards existence, and we perpetuate an elaborate and entrenched physical view as if it occupied the full extent of phenomena. Endeavoring to make sense of merely peripheral evidence that is estranged from the entirety, we envisage every imaginable explanation for an existence that is bereft of meaningfulness and purpose, without realizing that the essential significance of things does not reside in the blatant appearance.

Our perception is consistently directed towards the tangible aspects of phenomena because physical circumstances are readily verifiable while essential significance remains elusive to conventional cognition. Consequently, our entire understanding is distorted, and our relationship towards life is inevitably, physically excessive because we cannot grasp the manner whereby intrinsic significance as the meaningful substance of existence, can incorporeally endure.

Furthermore, our predicament is intensified because human, conventional, cognitive faculties fail to provide us with conclusive knowledge pertaining to intangible existence. They merely reveal a suggestion or an approximation of the elusive merit of circumstances while physical analysis, on the contrary, withstands all scrutiny and appears definite in all respects.

However, if existence were composed exclusively of matter, while meaning and purpose were merely negligible and without intrinsic significance, we would be justified in assuming that life was without qualitative pertinence or essential importance.

Unfortunately, the material condition of things has become our dominant perspective to the detriment of an entire dimension of intangible volume. Preoccupied with the obvious structure of things, we cannot grasp how or where intrinsic meaning could possibly exist. In this respect, both philosophy and religion fail us because, materially fascinated, we cannot conceive of an incorporeal existence that is of supposed, elemental priority. Consequently, we may find ourselves hoping that situations that would be irrational from a solely material perspective, might perhaps be authentic.

As long as the materialistic viewpoint and subsequent understanding remains exclusively oriented towards the superficial appearance of things, we come to regard all conditions merely in those limited terms. Thereby we sustain an indiscriminate ignorance of the meaningful value of existence because it is physically elusive and we dismiss its significance. Consequently, we uphold a disassociated, exclusively material perspective that we attempt to rationalize without convincing success because it contradicts experientially derived knowledge.

But physical conditions, disconnected from value and quality, are meaningless. Nevertheless, materialistic, Western philosophy claims that the opposite is the authentic state of things and this perspective has become implicitly entrenched within our perception of life.

In reality, the neglected, intangible dimension wherein meaningfulness, value and purpose resides, is of vastly substantial importance. The merely physical appearances of people and of material circumstances belie the essential substance of existence.

Fortunately, within the human, essential

constitution resides an elemental uniqueness that is our authentic identification. Akin to value, quality and meaning, it occupies the physically elusive status of immanent existence. Therefore, when we re-position our viewpoint away from the obvious, palpable properties of phenomena and engage them directly from the position of our own intrinsic, elemental significance we discover the magnitude of immanence wherein all that is profound and essential resides.

Immediately approaching circumstances from the perspective of the human, singular significance, we discover their intrinsic merit because our own essential consequence resides similarly within that same emphatic condition.

1. Immediate Cognition

Through the practice of immediate cognition, whereby we originally engage a situation or phenomenon without presupposition or anticipation; we are able to discover the essential distinction and condition of a particular situation. Conventional perception involves both rationalization and feeling evaluation, but the intellectually driven explanation of things is only the result of an oblique, corporeal function and feeling-sentience is always subjective and individually characteristic. Both practices fail to reveal the essential status of things because a conceptualization is an indirect agency of evaluation that does not expressly engage circumstances, while feeling evaluation is necessarily idiosyncratic.

A critical distinction exists between corporeally dependent comprehension through the somatic organs and faculties of the human constitution, and the direct approach of the singular individuation that occurs without intermediary evaluation.

Only the human being itself, as the uniquely individual distinction, is able to directly engage circumstances because it is not a corporeally dependent function but an extant entity. Consequently, through the imperative nature of our individual existence, we are able to recognize the intrinsic significance of all other things because we similarly exist emphatically and essentially.

The full, inherent volume of phenomenal existence including the human, unique distinction, is discovered through immediate cognition. Whenever we essentially engage phenomena and circumstances or recognize the human ipseity, we discover the incorporeal amplitude that is elusive to conventional cognition because of the circuitous and uncertain nature of rational apprehension. Furthermore, intrinsic identification does not lie in the physical condition of things but essentially. Therefore, through immediate cognition we encounter not merely the material appearance or the chronological status of things but the intrinsic pertinence.

For example, through familiar perception we observe an organism and readily recognize its physical condition. We endeavor to associate our impressions with prior acumen and further evaluate it upon the basis of our own particular bias.

But when we engage the creature from the perspective of our unique and essential distinction, we discover the intrinsic condition of its existence. Thus, we recognize the archetypal imperative that is the combination of the general principles that govern organic procedures and processes. These compel the organism through a metamorphic progression of growth and cyclical transformation. But we also grasp the particular, idiosyncratic disposition which is the qualitative manner whereby an organism is exceptionally expressed.

We find that the archetypal principle and foundation of organic organization exists as a mandate that commands the universal arrangement of the creature upon which basis it successfully functions. But every organism also expresses a cumulative, dispositional variation that compels its particular, physical stance and characteristic demeanor through response towards the influence of a changeable environment and the dynamic of that interaction.

Furthermore, the appearance of a life form is also determined by the greater ecological influences that impacts the form through physical and contextual restraints. Thus, the Blue Whale attains enormous proportions because the buoyancy of ocean water counters the pull of gravity.

Immediate cognition is original in the sense that it does not involve intellectual or feeling perceptive evaluation and interpretation. The human ipseity finds things as they exist inherently without the distortion and influence of antecedent assumption or subjective precedence. Consequently, through the immediacy of our approach, we discover the status of things as they exist of themselves and not as we presuppose or postulate them to be.

The human ipseity discovers itself through immediate, original experience and finds that its existence is unique. However, the intellect as a corporeal function is incongruous to the task of direct cognition because it cannot straightforwardly engage circumstances but must evaluate them rationally and indirectly.

That is to say, the intellect systematically calculates and enumerates information concerning a situation but it is unable to straightforwardly experience because the direct encounter is solely the prerogative of an entity. While the process of deduction is an obliquely operating function that is unable to definitively pronounce concerning the existence of the human ipseity and the intangible volume of phenomena because it is unable to substantiate elusive data. Thus, in terms of definitive confirmation, intellection is less consequential and argument is even further removed from the immediate event and rationale will always remain inconclusive through its inability to direct engage circumstances.

We imagine that through analysis, quantification and reduction, that we may deduce a degree of exactitude comparable to mathematical certainty. But even the most systematic and logical evaluation of things is far more fickle than numerical computation and more closely resembles jurisprudence than precise calculation.

Consequently, in order to discover the essential condition of the existence of something, it is crucial that the human entity itself immediately engage those circumstances and discover the imperative nature. Simultaneously, we restrain the interference of rationale and affective evaluation in order not to pollute the straightforward encounter through partisan assessment. Thereupon, the direct engagement of the human, essential ipseity with a phenomenon expedites the discovery of the elemental condition of its existence because the essential of the one recognizes the inherent distinction of the other.

2. The Intangible Merit of Things

The intrinsic, qualitative value and distinction of things are familiar even to casual experience, nevertheless, they are not considered of comparable significance compared with physical conditions and the obvious tangible properties of phenomena. However, essential significance cannot be precisely identified in the same manner that material conditions are scrutinized and further justified through calibration and quantification. Therefore, they are precluded from the materialistic, Western philosophical interpretation of existence, as if they were irrelevant. While not entirely maligned, they are treated with suspicion because they escape physical examination. Thus, we find ourselves with a slanted, philosophical perspective towards life that overemphasizes the palpable at the expense of intrinsic merit, a position that often extends into our interpersonal relationships.

Through exclusive emphasis upon the tangible evidence concerning things, we relinquish the signification, implication and the caliber of intangible, qualitative value, and fabricate an ideology that is void of meaning because it overlooks physically incompatible knowledge. This is because physical circumstances are blatant and readily rationalized because their properties are easily ascertained and verified. Furthermore, material conditions lend themselves conveniently to reduction and calculation with a mathematical efficiency that gives the appearance of subsequent, comprehensive knowledge and understanding, that is seemingly applicable across the entire spectrum of circumstances.

Through a preferential emphasis on the conspicuous properties of things, the authentic nature of existence is obscured through selective evaluation whereby we assume that everything of consequence must be physically substantial. But we cannot rightly claim to have decisively appraised existence when our approach neglects a significant proportion of the available evidence. To assert that circumstances are correctly assessed on the restricted basis of merely one cast of investigation is severely misleading and presents a contradiction between the common experience of the intangible merit of something and acumen derived from exclusively physical research.

This would matter less if an entire philosophical perspective had not been constructive upon purely material evidence. Thereby humanity lives according to a skewed perspective, with predictably peculiar results. It is as if we engaged circumstances only superficially, misunderstanding their actual nature and significance.

We do not deny the value of specialized knowledge, and we recognize that within the limited parameters of exclusively physical analysis, many discoveries are demonstrated as valid and significant through their practical application. But the approach whereby physically perceptible factors alone are considered the only pertinent consideration towards our understanding of existence, is misleading.

The express representation of phenomena upon the basis of their tangible properties is sufficient grounds only for an exclusively physical philosophy towards life. This is an untenable position because it is void of essential meaningfulness that is imperative to human, psychological amenity and, additionally, it contradicts knowledge that is derived from direct experience.

Furthermore, the assimilation of solely, conspicuous evidence and the analysis of the tangible conditions alone, inevitably leads to a world-view entirely derived from the extrinsic attributes of phenomena. Through a scrutiny of the purely tangible characteristics of things, we extrapolate our findings and manufacture an alien picture of existence. Thereby we disregard our own direct experience of the importance of the intrinsic value of circumstances because the essential distinction of phenomena is not amenable to physical analysis.

Additionally, we obstruct further research by an insistence upon the infallibility of meticulous, material research, deftly evading the fact that our source matter is entirely of a consistent, banal countenance because it excludes the consequential volume of things. Derived from the examination of solely material circumstances, our philosophical conclusions will be, inevitably, similarly arid.

The value and significance of phenomena exist in the intangible volume which is only obliquely reflected in the material conditions. Unfortunately, materialistic, Western philosophy has established a distorted ideology towards life that emphasizes the readily apparent as if existence were limited merely to the conspicuous properties of things. The resultant construct is without intrinsic significance because the qualitative value, the consequence and profound implication of material circumstances are unrecognizable through exclusively physical analysis. That is to say, the appearance of things consumes our attention with subsequent, recondite philosophical ramifications that are only sustainable through the denial of human experience to the contrary.

The immediate and original engagement of circumstances without partiality assumed precognition or foreknowledge, permits a straightforward, cognitive encounter whereby phenomena are discovered independently of human interpretation. We find things as they exist intrinsically and, consequently, we are able to determine their essential identification.

The direct engagement of a situation without penchant or preconception permits an original encounter to occur between the human entity and the phenomena. Consequently, through the restraint of rationale, the preclusion of conjecture and the interception of affective evaluation, an event of pristine cognition can occur that is entirely objective because it is without interpretative intermediary. Thus, the human, unique distinction directly experiences phenomena and discovers their essential condition of existence.

3. Qualitative Significance

In order to establish a dependable sensibility towards life, it is necessary to become familiar with the practice of immediate cognition and originally engage phenomena and circumstances. Thereby we become certain of what constitutes authenticity. Otherwise, we cannot conclusively distinguish between reality as a condition and a mere conviction that may or may not be substantively established.

The direct engagement of existence reveals the immanent volume wherein lies essential significance. In this way, through straightforward recognition, untarnished by explication or rationale, and uninfluenced by preference, we discover the elemental status of things.

Knowledge of the caliber of a particular, dispositional nature is elusive through rationale except in terms of the mathematical properties of things and their numerical interconnectivity. However, the computative aspects of phenomena do not comprise the entirety but merely those conditions that are amenable to quantification. Through an analysis of the mensurable parts, we do not discover the identification of something because we are solely occupied with the physics, mechanics and subsequent workings.

Upon the basis of the overemphasis of the quantifiable properties of things, a mechanical interpretation of existence has arisen that represents life solely in monotonous, technical terms. It is imagined that the function and operation of something determine the identification because only those quantifiable attributes can be conclusively confirmed and demonstrated to be authentic through physical analysis.

Exaggeration of the sensible particulars of phenomena is heightened because the qualitative significance of things is thought to exist under the same conditions as our subjective evaluation of them. It seems that we lack a manner of apprehension that is as correspondingly conclusive as our approach towards mensurable, physical properties. Therefore, we assume that intangible value is of lesser significance and somehow inconsistent because its acknowledgment and confirmation is dependent upon human, idiosyncratic evaluation. Consequently, the essential but physically elusive pertinence of phenomena is maligned as inconsequential unless it can be reduced in some way into calculable terms.

However, the intrinsic condition of things is not quantifiable because it does not exist tangibly. Consequently, that which is intangible yet experientially recognizable, such as the quality of something, is justified as being of a certain nature only through human consensus concerning a similarly shared experience. In other words, a quality does not possess definitive physical properties. If it did, it would be material and not elusive. Thus, the marginal material properties of a quality are only indirectly and distantly alluded to through quantification, but they cannot be essentially and entirely identified because mensuration only addresses those conditions that can be calibrated.

The essential and intangible volume of existence is where the identification, connotation and meaningfulness reside. The intrinsic and authentic distinction of something lies not in the functions, workings or physical properties but intrinsically. Similarly, the particular singularity of the human being does not intrinsically correspond with the corporeal structure and biological systems but exists essentially.

Through unfamiliarity, we assume that humanity is without the means to identify implicit and elementary inherency, except subjectively. But such is not the case. The human, intrinsic distinction exists within the same immanent volume as the inherent identification of all phenomena. Consequently, from the viewpoint of the essential ipseity, we are able to discover the intrinsic significance and profound identity of all other things.

Furthermore, engaging circumstances originally, we find ourselves inherently nourished because, unlike conventional perception, that which we discover consists of the entire identity of a phenomenon. In addition, when we encounter things from the viewpoint of our authentic identification, we become certain of our own particular and unique distinction. We recognize through immediate cognition that the significance of things exists immanently in a status of direct concurrence with our own signification. This then is the overlooked volume of meaningful existence, in the light of which the consequences of conventional perception and abstract conjecture appear merely superficial.

4. Conclusive Knowledge

In order to establish a relevant perspective towards existence that is not antagonistic but compatible with the way things are in reality, it is requisite to shape our approach upon conclusively confirmed knowledge. We need to condition our understanding upon certainty.

Conventional perception including intellectual rationale concerning the nature of existence, is alone unable to arrive at unambiguous knowledge because intellection hinders immediate engagement. That is, if an interpretative intermediary is established through deliberation it prevents the direct experience of phenomena and subsequent, essential recognition. Preoccupied by oblique exposition and circuitous reasoning, we assume that we can thereby achieve certainty with respect to the substance of life, when really we only rationalize about the nature of existence.

However, conclusive knowledge concerning the essential nature and identification of things is effectively accomplished when we engage circumstances directly and unequivocally. Through immediate cognition we find that we already enjoy the means whereby the distinctiveness of things may be emphatically ascertained. But the straightforward discernment of the intrinsic nature of phenomena remains entirely and inevitably contingent upon the similarly essential perspective of the observer.

The knowledge attained from a narrow materialistic view towards life will be inevitably, similarly limited. Predictably, if we seek only the workings and mechanics of things, our discoveries will be of the same kind. Therefore, if the shallow carapace is considered the full extent, human prospects would appear very grim because we would interpret life in those limited terms. However, it is through the obvious contradiction between a contrived ideology and our own personal experience to the contrary that we sense that exclusive materialism is a false proposition. In other words, restricted physicalism, founded upon the unperceptive premise that the obvious appearance of things comprises the entirety, even though a majority of people appear to tacitly accommodate it, concerns only the most superficial perspective.

We abdicate cognitive autonomy at our peril if we allow a plethora of humanly fabricated and confusing ideologies hold sway that merely detract from original engagement. Furthermore, there is no one but the individual who is able to directly engage circumstances and find the intrinsic merit of things. Thereby we discover for ourselves, upon the discovery of definitive knowledge concerning the status of existence, that we concomitantly command an essential wisdom when we recognize the intrinsic condition of circumstances. But all this remains beyond our reach if we permit someone else to explicate existence for us as a substitute for our own direct inquiry.

Immediate cognition is achieved through the impartial engagement of the perspective of the human, essential ipseity. Thereby, the human perspective becomes established straightforwardly from view of the intrinsic person. Consequently, once we recognize our distinct singularity, we find that we are no longer persuaded by aloof scholarship and contrived polemic but we reassess established and accustomed conjecture upon the basis of a direct experience of the elemental conditions of existence. We become familiar with the profound and we recognize the tenor of authenticity. Thus, we establish a benchmark of comparison against which ideological assertions and propositions may be tried for their legitimacy.

In early childhood, through innocence everything is encountered afresh before our impressions become contaminated through acquaintance and sophistication. In later life there often remains a nostalgia for those primal experiences and a longing takes hold to recapture the earliest experiences.

The forthright manner whereby an innocent child discovers the world through novel engagement is recovered through immediate cognition. In like manner we encounter circumstances originally although not through immaturity but by restraining the interpretative faculties and restricting associative coincidence. Thereby our encounter becomes direct and our experience original. Accordingly, we discover the intrinsic existence of things less through the enchanted eyes of childhood innocence but by a determined reorientation of perspective.

The intrinsic volume that qualifies the physical with meaning consists of the intangible assets of phenomena such as quality, intrinsic elemental identification and conceptual origin. Conversely, an investigation of the material structure or the analysis of the various components will not reveal the intangible substance because essential significance does not exist physically. In other words, chronology and magnitude are only pertinent to the corporeal condition, and they do not apply to intrinsic volume.

The poet and visual artist William Blake (1757-1827) painted what he famously termed *The Ghost of a Flea*. The picture measures only 8.42 inches by 6.3 inches but irrespective of the size of the composition, the essential disposition and qualitative complexion remains constant. If the painting were many times larger, the intrinsic content would remain the same. This is because the intangible volume that epitomizes the subject has nothing whatsoever to do with physical proportion. Furthermore, the eloquent depiction of the essential condition of something through the figurative and metaphoric articulation of the fine artist remains consistent regardless of duration. Blake's representation of the essential volume that identifies the particular nature of the flea endures obliviously through the passage of time in much the same way as the elemental identification of a particular color always remains the same.

William Blake (1757-1827)
Ghost of a Flea

5. Essential Identification

"I mean what I say," the Mock Turtle replied in an offended tone. And the Gryphon added, "Come, let's hear some of your adventures."

"I could tell you my adventures - beginning from this morning," said Alice a little timidly: "but it's no use going back to yesterday, because I was a different person then."

"Explain all that," said the Mock Turtle.

"No, no! the adventures first," said the Gryphon in an impatient tone: "explanations take such a dreadful time."

Lewis Carroll. The Gryphon in Alice's Adventures in Wonderland. Chapter 10

The effort that we make in order to properly appraise existence and subsequently align and appropriately apply ourselves towards our optimum advancement, is itself crucial to our development. For this reason we are not benefited if we allocate someone else to perform the work for us. It is ironic how humanity adheres to remarkably few doctrines and interpretations of existence and it is indicative of the passivity of the majority that so many thereby relinquish their self-determination.

Our goal is sovereign autonomy whereby the essential and singular human distinction assumes its rightful position as the authentic identification of our constitution because thereby we discover the intrinsic volume of everything else. Through materialistic, Western philosophy, humanity has become excessively identified with corporeal conditions at the expense of individual singularity and, consequently, we have come to deny the existence of our own incorporeal significance.

It is insufficient to tacitly endorse a philosophical or sectarian position and indiscriminately absorb doctrine and ideology on the strength of conviction because we thereby satisfy our uncertainty but we do not develop individual liberty. Hence, materialism, atheism and the abstract doctrines of contemporary science, including the theory of evolutionary caprice, are adopted through predilections in much the same manner as any other belief system or mythology. Upon very cursory examination, it is quickly evident that most establish their philosophical confidence on the strength of the acumen of others and not upon rigorous, personal research.

The discovery of the singular distinction of the individual as a fact of human existence is the task of every person to accomplish. It is not something that requires belief or even understanding but the recognition of incorporeal, individual uniqueness must necessarily be personally and experientially accomplished. Thus, ingenuity and acumen are essentially irrelevant to the immediate recognition of the human ipseity and abstract conjecture is merely a hindrance because it preoccupies our attention with speculative conditions. In other words, we must discover the human, essential distinction experientially.

Abstract rationale is the remote deliberation and imaginative extension of ideas that are not necessarily empirically demonstrated. Similarly, intellectual astuteness can never determine the human, essential distinction because the intellect operates subordinately to the ipseity and exists as a biological function. The essential human being is not an operation or an agency but a succinct and unique entity. Therefore, the significance of unique singularity is indeterminable through philosophical evaluation.

Immediate cognition is dependent upon the direct, experiential discovery of the human, unique ipseity and its positioning as the viewpoint and locus of our attention. If the conviction of restrictive, material exclusivity prevails, the motivation for direct, experiential research is forfeited. In other words, failure to maintain an open mind results in the preservation of the existing approach because the human ipseity must be directly acknowledged in order for humanity to progress towards cognitive autonomy. If we dismiss the existence of our own intrinsic identification, we also deny the ramifications of its establishment as our foremost point-of-view.

Nevertheless, rationale remains compelling because intellection through studied, sequential process appears confident. But logic is often mistaken for wisdom and the accomplished savant may become overconfident and indifferent towards an unconventional point-of-view dismissing that which appears counter to the established position and the accomplishments of their own mental adroitness.

The direct engagement of phenomena without intermediary interpretation shatters our enchantment with our own intellection, and we discover that we never really, unequivocally encountered circumstances before but only indirectly considered selected information. Immediate cognition enables us to experience things originally for their own merit and thereby discover their particular condition of existence. Furthermore, direct encounter establishes an original contiguity between the quintessential singularity of the observer and the elemental status of the object. Consequently, through immediate engagement we discover that we are able to discern the overlooked essential status of the existence of phenomena wherein all essential pertinence resides.

Conventionally, we endeavor to explicate circumstances based upon prior experience and conjecture and thereby we explain their significance through remote evaluation. We preoccupy ourselves with appraisal and content ourselves with our own estimation of phenomena. It matters less to us what things are in their own right and more significantly what we surmise concerning them. Thus, through deduction we never really determine the authentic status of something because our encounter remains remote from the actual circumstances.

Immediate cognition reveals the constitutional statement that epitomizes the essential identification of phenomena. The familiar approach is analytical and explicatory, and even through the most exhaustive, discursive industry we still fail to arrive at the ideal of the thing because intrinsicality is not indirectly determinable.

Phenomena proclaim what they inherently are through the immediate engagement of the human ipseity. Explanations take a very long time and fail in the end to approach the intrinsic distinction because the statement of the existence of something does not reside in the physical detail but concerns the essence of its existence.

6. Elemental Significance

The emphatic statement of the existence of something which we discover through the immediate, uncontaminated engagement of our unique and singular distinction, is its elemental identification. For example, the emphatic statement of a particular color is the consistent, representative ideal of that color. Thus, the color yellow has a particular and characteristic nature which the skillful artist may use intentionally to connote a certain condition or to express a singular value.

A particular tone of yellow may occur in flower and foliage, the mineral kingdom, the plumage of an exotic bird or in the rainbow. But wherever it is found it is always dependably of the same, distinctive caliber, irrespective of the context. The idiosyncratic quality of the color is its essential identification and it always makes the same, specific statement that proclaims its inherent distinction.

That which intrinsically characterizes yellow the artist uses to specifically enunciate the otherwise elusive viewpoint which is the essential substance of the painting. When the artist successfully combines the particular, elemental distinctions of a certain palette, a communication is achieved whereby the painting expresses a meaning that is beyond the mere admixture of pigment.

For instance, every color possesses a particular significance distantly analogous to the letters of the alphabet. The inherent cast and implication of every color is a characteristic elemental statement which is its intrinsic distinction and physically elusive identification. Thereupon, the fine artist may intentionally articulate a precise statement.

Similarly, every Native Element Mineral owns an idiosyncratic character that anticipates its physical composition and which represents its especial identification. The intangible, respective particularity that essentially epitomizes a specific mineral or color, is the constant, elemental distinction that is elusive to physical analysis because it is not found in its component, material parts.

Wherever a particular color or mineral is found, the idiosyncratic, essential identification is necessarily present but because it is not physically apparent, it must be discerned through immediate cognition. The elemental distinction that characterizes something exists in a permanent condition because unlike the physical representation, it resides immanently. In other words, the physical properties are dependent upon the intrinsic significance and not the reverse.

We assume that the authentic identification of something lies in the amalgamation of its particles and molecules and that through ever more refined and rarefied analysis we may discover its essential significance. But this is not the case. Through infinitesimal reduction we overlook the integrity of the entirety and instead we scrutinize the disposition of the detail which is something entirely different from the original object of our interest.

The discovery of the elemental significance and conceptual origin of things allows us to grasp the nature of the intangible volume of existence that is conventionally overlooked. We find in contrast to the physical, that the elemental, through its permanence, is the substantial condition of existence while the material status is essentially superficial because it is temporal and volatile.

Similarly, the human being possesses a corporeal, transient designation that disguises the immutable distinction that exists immanently and which is discovered through immediate cognition. The physical body belies the human, essential particularity that resides within the same volume wherein we find the elemental status of a color or the intrinsic identification of a mineral.

The determination to evaluate circumstances merely in physical terms and upon the basis of blatant appearances, denies the elusive knowledge that we can only ascertain empirically through direct engagement. That is to say, the subtleties of phenomenal existence such as value and quality are excluded from materialistically established philosophy and, consequently, the proposition of tangible exclusivity appears, against the results of our direct experience, contradictory and contrived.

The profound distinction of something, for example, does not enter into the restrictive, corporeal approach and, consequently, the narrow, material perspective appears partisan to us and strained when once we have glimpse the elemental significance of phenomena. Thus, materialistic philosophy seems fabricated and artificially sustained because it is obliquely conceived and abstracted from the actual event.

The establishment of a one-sided and partial improvisation as a feasible philosophy has disastrous consequences because it warps our understanding of existence and it is obstructive to human, cognitive emancipation. If we deny the existence of the human, essential condition and identify ourselves merely with the physical body, we relinquish all hope of significant, cognitive advancement because our further development requires the strategic repositioning of our authentic identification in order to immediately engage phenomena and discover their intrinsic condition. If we fail to discover our inherent singularity, we forsake the development of direct cognition wherein lies the certainty of human autonomy. Unable to discern the manner of elemental existence, we continue to perceive circumstances only superficially which amounts to cognitive censorship.

Our singular distinction of identification exists elementally and immanently, and it is through its unique perspective that we discover the essential circumstances of one another and that of phenomena. Within the experiential recognition of the elusive volume of existence resides the opportunity of human emancipation because thereby we discover things as they exist substantively and not merely ostensibly and apparently. With knowledge of the essential nature of existence, we are able to appraise circumstances judiciously because we ascertain their absolute status, which is not merely physical but profoundly intrinsic.

7. Immediate Engagement

The writings of French philosopher René Descartes (1596 – 1650), conceal an invaluable illustration of his respective struggle to reconcile the immediate cognition of the immanent volume of existence with the intellectual adjudication of circumstances. The enticing and optimistic assumption that dialectic methodology is analogous to the precision and efficiency of mathematical calculation, misled Descartes to suppose that the character of existence is successfully and conclusively determinable, solely through rationale.

By virtue of immediate, cognitive engagement, René Descartes discovered his own essential singularity, which is the human, incorporeally particular distinction. There is no other means whereby ipseity may be definitively identified. But he famously attributed his empirically ascertained findings to reason, characterized by the subsequently clichéd philosophical statement, *I think, therefore I am*.

But Descartes could not possibly have recognized his essential identification through rationalization or definitively corroborated its existence by exposition. The human ipseity is only unequivocally identified through direct experience. Unlike the precision of mathematical accountability, the resolve of the intellect pertaining to physically elusive existence, is insufficient. Reason cannot assimilate and conclusively deny or justify that which can only be experientially determined as extant.

Furthermore, through immediate encounter, Descartes similarly discovered the immanent volume of existence wherein all things exist essentially and without chronology or physical coordinates. This condition, through reverence and devotion, he characterized as Deity.

In other words, physically imperceptible value and essential existence are not convincingly determined by intellection because intangible evidence is neither reducible into mathematical terms nor demonstrable through argumentation. The intellect is a corporeal function that can speculate and imaginatively hypothesize, but it cannot experience and, consequently, it must indirectly deal with extracted data. In order to straightforwardly ascertain the intrinsic nature of something, calculation and judgment must be restrained to allow the human ipseity to directly engage circumstances without oblique, evaluative ambiguity and distraction.

Corporeal functions are incommensurate with human, essential ipseity because the former are organic instruments employed by the human entity while ipseity possesses emphatic existence and is capable of immediate engagement. Thus, the essential being is capable of direct, experiential cognition without the necessity of intermediary evaluation.

Descartes could not intellectually accommodate and reconcile forthright cognition with his conviction of intellectual infallibility through mathematically explicit methodology because the two are entirely disparate and incongruous. A significant undercurrent of contention is evident throughout his writings whereby he endeavors, by astute calculation to prove the validity of knowledge derived through immediate engagement but he fails in the task.

Thus, Descartes fluctuated between conviction concerning his own unique existence and that of Deity through the immediacy of his experience, and deliberate intellection that is constitutionally unable to fathom the physically elusive volume of existence. Consequently, as a man of integrity he frequently found himself unsettled and redetermined his position by reverting to those basic premises of which he was convinced. Accordingly, he justified the certainty of essential existence by direct encounter but was dismayed that his intellectual position appeared to contradict experience because he found that he could not decisively prove the existence of that of which he was most confident.

Moreover, Descartes attempted to delineate his thinking according to mathematical discipline. Imagining that he could rationalize and thereby decisively determine the nature of existence, he contemplated remotely from the immediate events that he had directly ascertained. The vastly profound significance of the immediate approach eluded him, and he became absorbed in abstract calculation assuming that if the premises were sound he could deduce the essential constitution of existence.

An intellectual premise is justified as valid only when it corresponds with immediately discerned reality. Otherwise, it exists in a vacuum, detached and unrelated to authentic existence. All manner of abstract speculation is pursued to its untenable conclusion when we fail to establish an absolute, experientially justified benchmark against which to qualitatively compare the merit of our speculation.

Had René Descartes recognized that his

discovery of unique ipseity and by extension, his direct knowledge of the essential, immanent volume of existence, might serve as a barometer of authenticity, his philosophy would have been entirely more suitably established. Instead, he attempted to position mathematical precision and exactitude as the emblematic bearings of his rationale but, unfortunately, numerical accuracy is not found even in the most systematic logical deduction. Nevertheless, he would have been able to correctly and conclusively evaluate the integrity of his thinking and avoid abstract, intellectual indulgence if he had been able to make the distinction between the computative confirmation of equations and existential quiddity. He drew an artificial parallel between mathematical precision whereby a correct solution may be discovered incrementally, with rationale that is always imprecise.

He thought that methodical, deductive exposition could prove that something was actual, but he confused the condition of actuality with that of incommensurate mathematical justification.

8. Organic Metamorphosis

Materialistic, Western philosophy considers existence merely from the narrow perspective of the indisputable, physical conditions and circumstances. Thus, it is hardly surprising that out of this meager doctrinal climate, a similarly slender evolutionary explication should arise that purports to illustrate the spontaneous origin of existence.

To the materialist, everything must possess an impetuous, reflexive antecedence because solely physical factors and attributes are permitted within the modern, exclusively corporeal, expository world-view. Even the fundamental building blocks of life that apparently possess merely electrical value, are necessarily, essentially physical in nature in order that they may be subjected to analytical scrutiny and encompassed within a materialistic ideology.

Moreover, it is an extraordinary thing, and indicative of the precedence and status of intellectual acumen, that so few interpretations of life proliferate. The world population is vast, but the majority of human kind fail to employ the necessary industry and determine for themselves the implication of their own existence. Consequently, from among a narrow assembly of popular alternatives we select a connotation that most closely symbolizes our personal proclivities but otherwise, very little original reflection occurs.

Thus, a situation has arisen in the West wherein only two general perspectives predominate: the religious and the scientific, with perhaps a third concession that vainly attempts to coordinate the antagonistic intensity of the main contenders.

The familiar Neo-Darwinistic evolutionary position rests upon the particular assumption that complexity may arise from biological rudiment if an almost infinite duration is conceded. Basically, anything can impulsively transpire if there is enough time. This convenient statistical artifice is partisan, not objective, otherwise it would similarly present the antithetical stance that timespan of itself is a non-creative condition and, consequently, it is not an admissible explanation for biological complexity. If endless continuance were excluded from the hypothesis then the insufficiency of the evolutionary argument would be blatantly self-evident. The pivotal controversy has nothing remotely to do with prolongation but very properly with the missing dynamic of impetuous ingenuity that apparently raises complexity out of simplicity.

Furthermore, the unlikelihood of the *Descent of Man* from a primitive origin is compounded when we explore and comprehend the distinctions between the biological kingdoms. The challenge to credulity is enormous when we attempt to clarify, not imaginatively and hypothetically but through scientific discipline, how the lower orders give birth to faculties that they do not themselves possess. If that were conceivable then the primordial would have to already embody in potential, the conditions of the higher orders.

Interestingly, this is precisely what happens in Nature. A seed that expands through metamorphic translation from a densely packaged embryonic condition into fruit bearing maturity, is not elementary but fully extant and equipped, albeit in a physically concentrated form. This is easier to understand when we view insect metamorphosis. The egg is not less consolidated than the caterpillar or at a more primitive stage than the chrysalis. When it suddenly leaps forward into the complexity of the butterfly, is does not evolve from spartan crudeness. The essential of the creature remains the same while the form structure and appearance change in order to complete a dynamic paradigm.

Architecture and appearance belie the consistency of the identification of the creature. We recognize metamorphic translation but, nonetheless, preoccupied with physical form, we abstractly fabricate an entirely antagonistic, evolutionary scenario and propose that organisms develop elaboration and complexity where before, none even remotely existed. Through immediate cognition we recognize the folly of conjectural formulation and how remote it can be from directly encountered reality.

The butterfly always exists in potential within the egg, the caterpillar and the chrysalis. Conversely, the egg or the caterpillar always exist in abeyance within the corporeal condition of the butterfly. Through a dramatic change in form, which is essentially contiguous with the consistency of identification, we recognize that the integral distinction of the butterfly is not physically, fully represented at any one time. Thus, we must concede that the butterfly designation exists in its entirety only intangibly, as an archetypal synthesis.

Similarly, the amphibian consecution through aquatic gill respiration towards lung breathing, does not imply that the frog evolved prehistorically from tadpole to land creature but merely that the particular metamorphic progression involves multiple ecological contexts. In the same way, the butterfly principle does not suggest that the flying insect evolved from the terrestrial or arboreal form but that earth, branch and air are habitats that correlate with its physical condition at different stages of its metamorphic progression.

Thus, the intriguing proposal that humanity arose from a primeval ocean eventually towards bipedal dominance of the Earth is dashed when we recognize that while creatures may assume flexible guises in order to reiterate the cycle of their development through different bionomics, the successive transaction itself is not capricious. Thus, the disposition and concomitant expression of a creature may adapt, but the intrinsic principle of cyclical recurrence remains consistent. Thus, we confuse the principle of organic, characteristic accommodation towards a changeable ecology, with an abstractly conceived evolutionary dynamic that does not actually exist in reality.

The human form is uniquely composed in that it does not possess the specializations that are peculiar to the animal. We do not have claws with which to dig but we can fabricate digging tools. An animal cannot do the same because its limbs are already specifically arranged for a particular mode of usage while our own remains generally dexterous. Through our versatility we may construct and fashion according to our needs and desires. But animal adroitness has very specific but limited application and it is obliged by its constitution to do things in a very certain manner.

The human being enjoys unspecified attributes, unlike the stipulated structure and organs of the animal. Thus, the terrestrial human could not arise impetuously

38

from an aquatic equivalent, because it does not possesses the same metamorphic flexibility of form that would allow it to physically modify to a different environmental milieu. The human being does not possess aquatic potential and it would be unsuited at any time for the ocean because it is without the specialized, transformative accommodation required for an oceanic ecology.

Growth is not merely expansion but the dynamic translation of appearance through a cyclical progression. Nowhere in Nature can form evolution be found where an alternative condition did not already exist in potential. The fabricated, abstract concept that suggests that animals and plants arose from a primitive origin into sophistication is uncharacteristic in Nature. But what is evident is the existence of an archetypal establishment wherein the conceptual entirety of a creature is never concurrently evident but nonetheless exists intangibly in its completeness.

The essential conflict that motivates and impels the strife between those who support a Darwinist explanation of existence and the Creationist, is more mundane than it appears. Both positions are uncertainly authenticated convictions. The one is atheistic while the other is plainly theistic and in this partiality lies the real contention. The Darwinist may claim the methodical, scientific approach but in reality the evidence is consistently circumstantial and distorted by the desire to demonstrate an already sanctioned position. Darwinism is a philosophy like any other, and not a science.

When we directly engage phenomena, we set aside ambiguous conjecture in order that the human, essential ipseity may become the locus of our perspective. We meet things straightforwardly and thereby discover their particular condition. In other words, we discern what is actually occurring when we encounter circumstances through unique and impartial cognition.

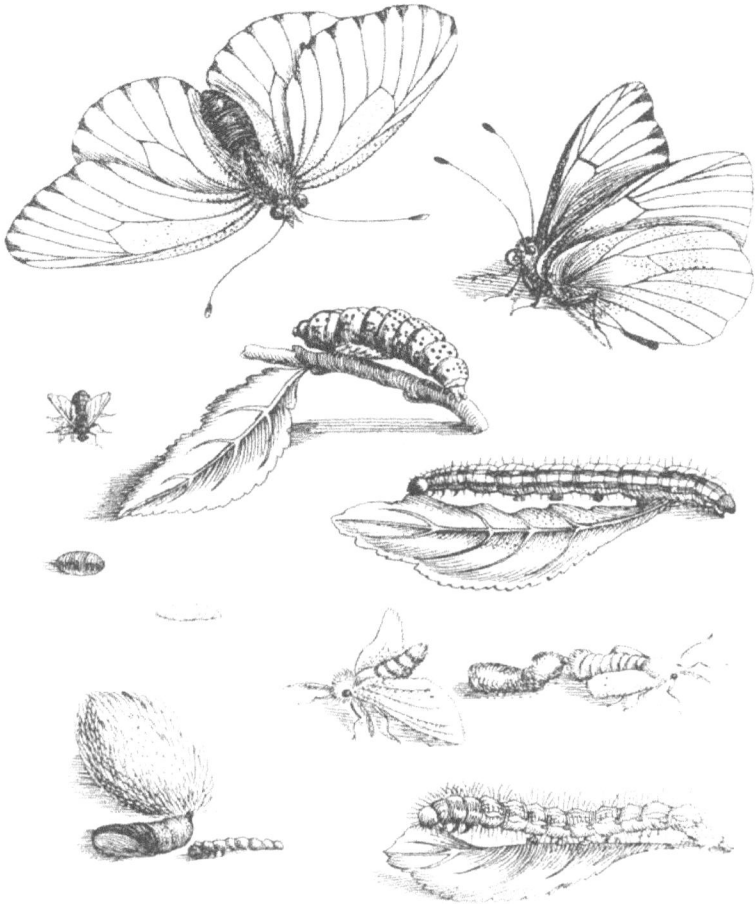

The butterfly designation exists in its entirety only intangibly, as an archetypal synthesis, or over time as a cyclical progression of appearances.

Plate by Maria Sibylla Merian (1647 – 1717)

9. The Meaningful Volume of Existence

There is no alternative dimension, celestial paradise or great beyond. Inevitably, we reside within the confines of a limited mentality which restricts our perception. While that which hinders our view is our own immaturity, both moral in the sense of egotistical circumscription, and cognitively in terms of our superficial and oblique viewpoint and the unmindful manner of our consideration of existence.

Acknowledgment of the absence of an ethereal, refined physical-condition or location does not justify the myopic perspective of materialistic, Western philosophy. It merely returns our attention to our prevailing circumstances and thereby we avoid abstract supposition which is of no particular value to us because it is both gratuitous and misleading.

Intricate but abstruse calculation may appear to establish the conceivability of alternative dimensions but upon careful scrutiny we discover that the original concepts upon which they are founded are merely hypothetical and only tenuously supported. The conditions that illustrate a certain postulate are often not attainable in reality. Thus, any interaction that is imagined at the speed of light has no practical value for us and merely exists as conceptual ingenuity.

In is unfortunate that we find abstraction so compelling but is hardly surprising. If we disclaim the existence of the human, essential distinction and attempt to attribute the significance of things to their physical characteristics, much concerning our own identification remains enigmatic and perplexing. If we rob our experiences of their intangible significance then we effectively impede the recognition of the meaningful volume of life. Consequently, we speculate, endeavoring to establish a plausible explanation concerning existence. Thus, we delve deeper into the tangible circumstances of things at the expense of developing intrinsic acquaintance wherein lies the overlooked connotation and essential magnitude.

When we immediately and originally encounter circumstances, we discover the elemental status and meaningful volume. Directly experiencing something from the viewpoint of our own essential distinction is liberating because it requires the appointment of our own extraordinary uniqueness as our cognitive authority. Thereby, we engage circumstances without the intermediary of intellect or of affected interpretation and we discover both our own significance and that of the particular subject of interest.

Thus, two vital transactions occur. We recognize our own singularity, and secondly from that viewpoint, through the direct application of our attention towards other circumstances, we thereby discover their physically elusive, essential overtone.

The greater, meaningful volume of existence resides in a condition of immanence of which we are unfamiliar because we customarily negotiate with the incontrovertible, physical prominence of things. Through immediate cognition, the human, incorporeal, unique distinction directly experiences that outstanding, essential expanse. We find that everything possesses intangible measure of which we were formerly unaware because we concerned ourselves principally with the corporeal semblance.

Of paramount hindrance is the indirect, oblique manner of thinking that we have become accustomed to. We calculate, evaluate and speculate constantly, corroborating our deliberations with accumulated, antecedent associations and influencing our reflections through visceral discrimination. The circuitous assessment of circumstances consumes our attention, and we imagine that we have correctly identified something when we only comprehend its ostensible significance.

Ordinarily, we do not allow the circumstances to speak for themselves whereby we may learn of their authentic status but we graft our own supposed acumen and analytical camber in substitution. Consequently, we are without original knowledge and we merely deceive ourselves, imagining that which we suppose we know is more pertinent that the extant condition of a thing that exists independently of our opinion.

If we imagine things to be other than they really are, we will acquit ourselves according to the texture and parameters of our convictions. We ingeniously encourage and increase our confusion, and our deceptive perspective becomes peopled with additional elaboration compounding the original misperception. Thus, we look to those who possess elite scholarship and expect to find perceptibility and transparency but beyond the erudite repetition of an extant philosophical position, seldom do we discover significant wisdom.

To imagine that we possess knowledge concerning essential existence and maintain an explication of life founded upon conceptual comprehension, is sadly misleading. We only discover the authentic status of something when we engage it directly without pre-deliberation. In other words, knowledge of the intrinsic, essential profundity of existence is elusive to rationale but, nevertheless, therein lies the authentic account. It is small wonder that the philosophical intelligentsia fiercely resists the concept of obtaining existential knowledge through direct cognition because it implies that it is accessible to everyone and not merely the monopoly and domain of academic or religious authority.

10. The Self-Circumscribed Mentality

Progress in the practice of immediate cognition, whereby we discover the essential, intangible significance of things, requires application. It is not achieved merely through intellectual understanding. The recognition of the incorporeal, elemental volume of phenomena and a subsequent distaste for the superficial perspective that restricts us to the hidebound and commonplace, must be actually attained or it merely remains a conceptual potential.

However, even though we directly experience our authentic identification and establish the human, essential ipseity as our viewpoint, our position remains uncertain if we yet retain an antecedent and obsolete demeanor. There will always exist a conflict and although we strive to discern the intrinsic distinction of phenomena and maintain an essential perspective, transformation of character is not accomplished merely through human will and determination.

Character cannot effectively self-ameliorate, and earnestness of itself is insufficient because we do not possess the necessary alternative paradigm to replace egocentrism. Furthermore, we cannot realistically conceive of a substitute and regardless, even if we could, our self-circumscribed nature would inevitably hinder its accomplishment. The petty sense-of-self apprehensively equates the renunciation of its significance with dereliction.

We cannot establish the human, essential ipseity as our sovereign identity and simultaneously retain our self-circumscribed mentality. It would be as if we possessed two contradictory natures. The petty sense-of-self is only significantly reassured through immanent, supernal influence within the human heart itself. Thereupon, we surrender existential apprehension and we are heartened through an intimate concurrence with supernal caritas.

The immanent intangible volume of existence is discovered through the direct engagement of the human, essential ipseity. Within that same compass also resides the surrogate principle that replaces the human, obsolete mentality and permits the establishment of our intrinsic distinction.

But the approach to matters that concern human character and temperamental circumstances, is not through reason or determination, but by openhearted sincerity because it is within the heart that self-centeredness is implicated. The supernal expediency that resolves self-ambiguity resides within the physically elusive volume of immanence but our approach must be through concurrence within our own heart.

Comparable to the authentication of the significance of immediate cognition as the means of to discovering the inherent distinction of things, the verification of the transformative influence of supernal caritas is only possible through its implementation. It is neither confirmed nor contradicted by intellection or affective evaluation.

It is within our deepest nature that the obsolete, self-preoccupied mentality is established as a misidentification. The intellect itself is not self-centered because as a function it does not possess the singularity of an entity. Thus, character is not found within a physical

48

organ but resides intangibly within the human psyche.

The manner whereby the mentality of self-circumscription is rendered vulnerably towards reorientation is sincerity. It is senseless to recite invocations, to plead and cajole because these practices are ineffective and merely reveal wistful ignorance. These things are the debris of a superstitious mentality and, consequently, they are unable to address the essential necessity of a dispositional transformation because they remain as an entrenched aspect of the human predicament.

The temporary and perishable nature of our corporeal condition is self-evident to us all. Thus, we recognize from the moment that we become aware of the deficiency of the self-circumscribed mentality, that rendering ourselves vulnerable to supernal caritas is both crucial and opportune. We only have to glance about us to determine the dire consequences of futile egotism and its hapless ramifications.

Upon the practice of immediate engagement, we inevitably recognize with certitude that the essential ipseity offers cognitive liberty in terms of discovering the intrinsic meaningfulness of existence. But the confirmation of our own quintessence and that of others, is also tremendously significant in its further implication because it indicates an essentially distinct, overlooked volume beyond the merely physical status of things. Furthermore, it reveals where the significant essential of things is to be found. We discover the domain of immanence.

But human immodesty and fundamental misidentification contradict the establishment of the essential ipseity and distort the results of our exploration, through audacity and conceit. Consequently, our existential uncertainty yearns for assurance and seeks self-aggrandizement as a substitute. Moreover, in terms of dispositional reorientation, we do not know what an essentially selfless, constitutional paradigm looks like and the appeal of elaboration and embellishment is captivating because of our basic insecurity.

The condition of the heart and its particular inclination determines and predisposes our perception of existence and subsequent experience. Therefore, it is essential that the heart be reestablished upon a substantial and realistic foundation otherwise the inevitable ramification of self-circumscription is anguish through the maintenance of a fractious and defensive disposition. Our task is to make the heart amenable to restoration through straightforward sincerity and vulnerability towards the supernal caritas that occupies the immanent volume of things.

Old Man in Prayer
Opening the heart involves a combination of
vulnerability and receptivity towards supernal caritas.
Rembrandt van Rijn - (1606 –-1669)

51

11. A Benchmark of Reality

There is a cognitive approach towards circumstances that does not involve idiosyncratic evaluation, intellectual assessment or rely upon the precedency of prior acumen. It is a manner of engagement that occurs straightforwardly between the human, essential identification and a phenomenon. The unique distinction that epitomizes and distinguishes human singularity exists incorporeally and, consequently, it is able to discern the intangible, intrinsic significance of all other things.

Physical conditions do not comprise the entirety of phenomena nor do they approach the essential implication but they represent solely the superficial perspective. Abstractly isolated by a materialistically exclusive philosophy, mundane properties are unnaturally dissociated from their meaningful volume and subsequently appear nonsensical. Thus, our attention is absorbed by a merely partial aspect of existence and all the scrutiny and analysis of the outward circumstances can never reveal the essential substance because crucial meaning does not reside in the physical minutiae. The corporeal condition of things is the consequence of an intangible origin.

The direct engagement of circumstances and people reveals their authentic status and significance because we encounter things from the viewpoint of our own intrinsic principal that exists elementally. Furthermore, we thereby establish a familiarity with that which constitutes the entirety of things. The overlooked volume also includes the conceptual origin of organic organization as well as the particularity of substances and the distinction of essentially intangible phenomena such as colors.

The immediate experience of essential conditions establishes an independent standard of that which constitutes the full spectrum of reality. Thus, we readily distinguish between authenticity and abstractly contrived, fabricated or imaginary interpretations of existence.

Through oblique, cerebral calculation, rational deduction and justification based upon the solely peripheral evidence of phenomena, we can only indirectly appraise a situation. Intellection, as an organic function, is without singular identification and, consequently, it is incommensurate with the essential, human being because it is an operation and not an individual. Only the human principal can directly engage circumstances and discover the essential significance of things because we exist emphatically.

Similarly, the brain or any bodily organ does not possess human individuation except in the abstract imagination of the theorist who has failed to discover personal significance and attributes identity to the temporal faculties. The distinction between an organic apparatus and the human, essential host who applies calculative rationale to a situation becomes confused through an abstruse intellection that supposes existence to be exclusively physical.

A similar confusion exists between the exactitude of demonstrably justified mathematical calculation, with conclusively determined knowledge regarding the authentic condition of things. Precise accounting does not reveal existential reality. The two have nothing in common because they are disparate conditions without mutual correspondence. This entanglement of incompatible values leads us to suppose that the physics of phenomena may reveal their intrinsic identity which only compounds our preoccupation with the notion of material exclusivity.

Feeling-sentient evaluation is an opposite approach to cerebration. The essential ipseity as the human, unique distinction is similarly overlooked and, consequently, without the direct engagement of the individual principal, subjective knowledge remains merely indeterminate. That is to say, affective evaluation is without the conciseness of systematic deduction and being unpredictable it is incommensurate with certainty in the same manner as abstract rationale but without inherent, logical constraint. The moderation of the emotive evaluation of circumstances rests upon workaday commonsense.

In practice, both approaches overlap and rationale influences balmy intuition while cold calculation is ameliorated through levity and impulsiveness. But neither expedient offers conclusive knowledge concerning the intrinsic nature of things because the human principal is not positioned as the sovereign, cognitive perspective. Of an entirely different value, the essential ipseity engages circumstances directly without calculation or interpretative fancy. It is through the immediacy of the encounter that definitive, existential comprehension is obtained. Thereby, nothing impedes the acquisition of essential knowledge.

Without direct experience through the human, essential ipseity, we overlook the intrinsic volume of existence which is the realm of reality. We remain at the mercy of every convincing rationalization or appealing reverie and we inhabit an assumed condition that varies with each individual. We are without a benchmark that indicates definitive reality and cannot distinguish between deception and authenticity. Furthermore, through immediate cognition, we find that there is no such thing as unreality beyond the theoretical concept of an opposite condition to extant existence. The only real circumstances are the authentic way things actually are. The rest is delusion.

12. The Physically Circumscribed Mentality

It should not seem extraordinary, that when we encounter phenomena directly through the human, essential ipseity, that we find them entirely differently represented than the manner in which we customarily recognize them. Formerly, we perceived things in what we imagined were their authentic status of existence but now we find that our perspective was merely superficial. When we engage circumstances uniquely they assume an entirely more meaningful countenance than when we consider them obliquely, subjectively or imagine that we know what they are through prior association with similar situations.

The elemental condition of things that we discover when we experience them from the viewpoint of our essential identification, is the authentic circumstances of their existence. When we recognize the entirety of something through the direct approach, we find that we become subsequently alert to what constitutes the wholeness. The blatant, physical conditions are insufficient because they offer only incomplete evidence that is gleaned from an examination of merely the conspicuous aspects. In order to discover the entirety of the existence of something, all the evidence must be taken into consideration including intangible significances, otherwise our cognition cannot be considered conclusive.

The intangible significance of phenomena is not readily discernible through conventional cognition and cannot be discovered through a scrutiny of solely the material conditions. Furthermore, while experiential engagement reveals the existence of the elusive, essential substance of things, usually their interpretation and description are characteristically influenced by the idiosyncratic perception of the individual observer. Consequently, inconstant testimony is capricious, and its pertinence is frequently overlooked because the assessment of intangible value differs with each person.

This seems to be an unsolvable quandary because definitive knowledge appears accordingly unattainable through the limitations of our human, constitutional resources. Thus, we struggle for decisive apprehension through the consideration of one-sided intelligence which is readily verifiable and easily demonstrable as authentic.

Thereby, our entire understanding is almost exclusively derived from the physical condition of things. Consequently, our viewpoint is superficially skewed, and we imagine that the entirety consists solely of the material circumstances. Was it not for the extraordinary human capacity of direct cognition we would be unable to escape the presumption that the obvious appearance comprises the entire significance of existence and that anything physically elusive we must uncertainly attribute to a vague mysticism.

Through the practice of immediate cognition by the human, essential distinction, we establish a barometer of what constitutes reality whereby every hypothesis can be tried and ascertained for its congruity through qualitative comparison. Thus, we are not misled into accepting what is merely conjecture or conviction even though the persuasive rhetoric of the proponent may seem convincing. We know the tenor of reality, and we cannot be deceived by speculation.

The human plight is dire, and the moment is crucial to recognize that we subsist under a profound deception that works entirely against our own best interest. There is a congenital discrepancy between empiricism and abstract evaluation. Increasingly, we have come to accept a philosophy that is established entirely upon depthless evidence. This inevitably condemns the phenomenon of our own individuality to irrelevance because we philosophically conclude that we are just another body among a legion. Furthermore, through the denial of all but material circumstances, we muster information concerning existence solely from that same perceptible extension. Thus, we compound the abstractly established delusion that the appearance represents the whole of existence.

The assumption that we are merely somatic because we are unable to corroborate through physical means that which we know experientially concerning the elusive volume of circumstances, is paradoxical. We accept the hollow interpretation but remain troubled by reservations that we cannot substantiate.

Through, an excessive preoccupation with the semblance of things, we arrive at the moribund conclusion that the carapace of existence comprises the entirety. This predicament is compounded when we attempt to substantiate our suspicions through rationale because deduction functions ideally with tangibly verifiable evidence and, consequently, specious dispute is easily overwhelmed. Thus, we inevitably conclude that our human condition is similarly superficial.

The assumption that the essential, human

distinction is merely temporal and perishable is a profound misconception with ominous ramifications because it condemns us to a physically circumscribed mentality that is without panacea. But the viewpoint of the unique, individual ipseity permits us to discover for ourselves the authentic nature of existence. Through immediacy, without the hindrance of intellection and affection, our encounter becomes original and entirely without idiosyncratic subjectivity or abstract speculation. We directly confront circumstances from the sovereign perspective of our authentic identification and thereby discover the overlooked, essential volume of existence that cannot be otherwise, physically determined.

13. The New Paradigmatic Disposition

Through the denial of the existence of a human, unique individuality that is corporeally independent, we obstruct our own maturation and flourishing. An inevitable immorality towards one another becomes acceptable, and we decline towards callousness and crudity because we seem to exist essentially without consequence. Ironically, we assume that the material conditions comprise the substantial constituent of existence, while in reality we only recognize and consequently occupy the least meaningful periphery unless we reposition our perspective.

Furthermore, there is nothing within material, sensible circumstances that can nourish the intrinsic human being and gratification must be endlessly repeated in order to assuage the famishment. Otherwise, we can only deflect an essential agitation through preoccupation and distraction. Corporeality, through the abstract artifice of Western, materialistic philosophy, is extracted and sublimated from the full volume of existence and exclusively emphasized. But the physical is only the superficial aspect that, disengaged from the entirety, appears to be without origin, objective or meaning. Therein, the essential human being finds little consolation.

Of commensurate importance to the recognition of the human, unique distinction is the amelioration of an obsolete, egotistical orientation. The assumption that the petty sense-of-self possesses consequence is the origin of considerable human antagonism. In order to avail ourselves of remedial reorientation, it is essential to situate oneself in concurrence with an extraneous influence because the human mentality does not possess dual psychology and cannot effectively redress its own fundamental predisposition.

Reformative goodwill and wisdom do not reside within the physical conditions of things but within the essential volume. The task is to permit an inspired mentality to supersede the mundane. This is a constant activity that soon becomes second nature because the former self-circumscribed demeanor rapidly appears abhorrent and uncouth to us from the perspective of the new.

Through openhearted sincerity, a new paradigmatic disposition is steadily established that is without the egocentrism of the petty sense-of-self. But the manner of ingress is not through the intellect nor by imagination but it is at the seat of the affections where the remediation must occur. Thus, an exemplary frame of mind becomes our own condition through openhearted concurrence. It arises within the heart because the heart is the locus of our predilection and, consequently, it is where essential reorientation must take place. Thereby, we not only inaugurate right-mindedness but establish a constitution that is qualitatively consonant with the supernal nature.

Openhearted sincerity towards supernal caritas requires that we effect a posture of receptivity and willingness to embrace a new and antipodal disposition. We permit ourselves to a reorientation of demeanor and allow ourselves to be nurtured towards a new complexion. We do not try to self-educate or suppose that upon the strength of our own merit and acumen we can self-ameliorate but we accommodate the transformation through receptivity.

Conversely, we are mistaken if we imagine that through our own sensibility we can sustain a benevolent demeanor. If we try to fashion our version of graciousness, we will find that the resultant character has yet remain self-circumscribed. In an analogous sense, it is as if the caterpillar were to attempt to become a butterfly through strength of will. Determination is entirely misapplied if we suppose thereby that we can reorient ourselves because we cannot conceive of that essential, prototypical temper nor effect the necessary dispositional transposition.

We open the heart and through vulnerability, we accommodate a profound reconstitution. This essential stance permits the investiture of a crucial and foundational reestablishment. However, it is less a matter of individual extension but more significantly, one of welcoming the metamorphic transformation of our obsolete disposition through affinity and willingness. We permit the cultivation of a new mentality through a change of heart thereby a far greater goodness accomplishes the change itself and it is to this that we make ourselves receptive.

It is important to return to the locus of the heart when we find ourselves in conflicting circumstances. Lasting reorientation only transpires when it is accomplished by supernal caritas and if we imagine that we can establish the new paradigm within our psyche through our own good intention, we misjudge the immensity of the task. Thereby, we easily become confused through mental and emotional commotion which only compounds our disquietude. Regardless, eventually, with familiarity we will naturally desire to seek supernally inspired reorientation because we develop confidence in the dynamic of character reconstitution.

It is an enormous relief to relinquish our obsolete mentality in hushed wholeheartedness and welcome the cathartic reformation of the human psyche upon an entirely different basis to our former, petty sense-of-self. Through openhearted sincerity, an appropriate mien deposes clamorous uncertainty and we experience renewal through sublime instruction. This occurs to us within the condition of openhearted immediacy because supernal caritas occupies that place of immanence wherein the significance of all things resides.

The School of Guido Reni (1575 – 1642)
The Madonna at Prayer

65

14. Existential Liberation

Emotional euphoria is a poor substitute for an essential, dispositional reorientation. Through excitement we may attain self-induced mystical exhilaration but frenzy and transport have no correlation with human, paradigmatic regeneration. We cannot compare abandon and overwrought passion with openhearted concurrence whereby we unpretentiously welcome intrinsic reestablishment.

It is vital that we approach the necessity of human soul-transformation realistically. Overtones of mysticism or magic are unhelpful. Otherwise, we merely add to an already confused and misunderstood approach, with further ignorance. We distort the contingency of remediation which is an imperative and indispensable necessity, and we make it seem ludicrous through trivial misconstruction.

Therefore, we survey the human plight with unequivocal deliberation and accordingly we affirm the causality and remediation of our predicament. We find self-circumscription to be the antithesis of sovereign liberation because through the illusion of disassociation, egoism inevitably furthers existential apprehension and subsequent defensiveness.

Our goal is to awaken the human, essential ipseity which is our authentic identification. But we cannot self-transform an inherent conviction of estrangement and personal isolation. The petty sense-of-self will consistently hinder our attempts because it is convinced that within the condition of physical segregation lies our authentic prerogative.

This is a significant deception of the self-absorbed mentality and the origin of subjective anxiety. We are persuaded of the certainty of this position through the perspective of the separate, corporeal body that we imagine is the entirety of our existence. We are ignorant of immanence wherein the meaningful volume of existence resides and consequently we remain convinced of existential separation in the manner of the physical condition.

Soul-transformation requires identification with an entirely different perspective from the partitioned mentality that originates from corporeal circumstances. We directly experience the manner of essential existence through openhearted sincerity and we permit the meaningful viewpoint to assume precedence over the distortion of apportioned segregation.

We discover that the circumstances of essential existence and of subsequent meaningfulness, exists not in spatial isolation but in immanent concurrence.

The reorientation of our moribund mentality is, therefore, requisite because the disjointed and insular mindset that dominates our psyche is without value or future. It does not resemble essential existence but merely assumes prominence through the accumulated conviction that the human distinction simulates our physical confinement.

We do not possess the capacity to self-ameliorate and mitigate the intensity of misidentification. The petty sense-of-self never surrenders its status, but it merely assumes an alternative guise. Thus, our sole identification appears to be confined within an uncertain and transient character, anxious for its survival.

Soul-transformation of the caliber that is imperative to existential liberation occurs only through supernal concurrence. It is established through openhearted sincerity because it is within the heart that the predicament of uncertainty arises. Otherwise nothing substantial can occur and the metamorphic transformation of the human psyche from egocentrism to sovereign autonomy remains remote.

The envisioned relinquishment of self-circumscription through induced excess, jubilation or by strength of will and determination, much like the belief in a blissful hereafter, merely detracts our attention. What is essential is a quiet susceptibility of the utmost profoundness whereby the open heart aligns itself with supernal caritas and thereby becomes reoriented according to the exemplary quality of the supernal disposition.

Through receptivity, we find our former estranged status superseded by assurance, and we adopt a befitting and realistic mentality that essentially reestablishes our frame of mind. We relate to existence as it really is and not as we presume or imagine it to be. We find that intrinsic identification is not segregated and separate in the manner of physical conditions but exists within the unanimity of coincidence. This discovery is corroborated through immediate cognition. We discover that inherent existence is of an entirely different status than the physical circumstances which are merely the terminal condition of things.

The material aspect of existence is the most obvious countenance. But it cannot exist separately from the intangible volume because isolated it possess no value and it is rendered meaningless. Similarly, the human, physical condition is merely the superficial facet of the intangible, unique identification that exists in an immanent correspondence to the essential of all other things.

The error of perception that induces us to emphasize merely the blatant appearance of phenomena disassociated from their inherent establishment, is countered through supernal influence. The greater compass becomes known through openhearted sincerity, and we recognize the essential of things including the incorporeal singularity of ourselves and others. This establishes an entirely different correlation between people because intrinsic identification discovers a similarly fundamental particularity akin to our own significance. Thus, all correspondence becomes meaningful and we find that to do harm hurts ourselves with a reciprocal intensity. Subsequently, we relinquish self-circumscription for modesty and deference because egocentrism becomes abhorrent to us. We disdain self-centeredness because it is antagonistic to our authentic identification.

15. The Simplicity of Openhearted Sincerity

We are able to differentiate between our essential singularity and our corporeal circumstances through the dispassionate observation of sensation. By means of objective attention, we observe physical impressions and through the act of surveillance we demonstrate that we exist independently of the body. If the body were the entirety of our existence, we would be unable to detach from it and we would be helpless to describe a sensation in impersonal terms because objectivity necessitates dual identification.

Similarly, we can monitor the commotion of the intellect. Impressed by the clamorous affections, it perpetually vacillates between the premise and proposal endeavoring to attain a satisfactory resolution. Consequently, we find that it is far more preferable to indwell the heart and anticipate the silent nurture of supernal beneficence than to endure the incessant bedlam of rationalism.

Through the impersonal audit of sensation, mental calculation and of the affections, we become certain of a particular distinction that is disassociated from the body. This is our sovereign identification that must become positioned as our cognitive viewpoint in order that we may engage circumstances immediately without corporeal intermediary.

The human, unique distinction is an impalpable entity that resides in a condition of immanence with the essential significance of all things. Immanency is quite unlike physical ambiance and once we have directly encountered it, we recognize the banality of the philosophy of material exclusivity because we confirm the impossibility of independent material circumstances, void of meaningful origin.

Furthermore, recognizing our own unique and incorporeal distinction, we find that our essential identification requires far more substantial sustenance than that available through the gratification of physical appetites which must be endlessly repeated. Dissociated from our imperative, incorporeal uniqueness we find ourselves in circumstances that are bereft of meaningfulness and purpose. However, it is upon these two consequential principles that the human, intrinsic entity is sustained.

The human, essential ipseity is able to immediately engage all phenomena and discover their particular distinction. This is also true in respect of sound whereby a particular cadence is found to possess singular meaning not only in reference to its origin but, as every musician knows, akin to the precise connotation of a language. Thus, the painter uses color in order to reveal intangible content, while the musician paints with sound.

This is possible because the characteristic essential of something reveals more distinctly its identity than the physically discernible parts are able to portray. For this reason, the authentic existence of something is lost when we assume that we can discover what it is through mere quantification. All that we attain is knowledge of those obvious properties that are amenable to calculation and, consequently, the intangible volume of something which alone possesses the value and meaning, remains elusive.

Immediate cognition requires the restraint of intermediary interpretation in order that the human, essential identification may discover its own existence through direct, experiential engagement. However, this demands discipline and determined practice which is inevitably the approach of an exclusive few because only a minority recognize its ultimate value.

However, openhearted sincerity is supremely simple and merely requires our straightforward compliance. We do not have to perform the transformation ourselves and, indeed, we find that the human psyche is unable to self-ameliorate but must relinquish authority to far wiser ministration. Consequently, susceptible willingness renders the heart openly towards the forces that facilitate and further the appropriate transformation.

The process of conversation from a mentality of self-circumscribed isolation towards magnanimity and inclusion is markedly practical and enormously to our advantage. We lose nothing of intrinsic value, and we merely relinquish an erroneous, contrived conceptualization that fabricates a false identification.

When once we assent and begin to defer to supernal caritas, we never desire to return to our former moribund mentality but we seek to embrace the new. Constantly, we choose between the antecedent inadequate mindset of self-circumscription, and we eagerly align with the new paradigm. Steadily, a vastly refreshing viewpoint and dispositional soundness are established within the heart, which is the new human archetype.

The recognition of our own incorporeal, unique

distinction, that of others and, subsequently, the elemental status of phenomena, enables us to anticipate and apprehend conditions that are not circumscribed by physical circumstances. Thus, aware of a greater volume to existence than mere appearances, the segregated, petty sense-of-self becomes acutely alert to its own ignominy. Astonishingly, through open-hearted sincerity, we discover that we are merely at a subordinate stage of our development which forthwith becomes distasteful to us and we yearn to progress. Thereby, we discover, through unaffected earnestness that the means of our advancement is already, inherently established and merely awaits our participation.

The manner whereby we avail ourselves of the transformative influence of a supernal corrective is through guileless candor because it is the status of our foundational mentality that requires reexamination. Our part is make the heart continuously accessible in order that a progressive, revolutionary mindset may supersede egocentrism.

16. From Self-Concern to Impartial Magnanimity

The recognition of one's own unique existence is pivotal towards the explicit discernment between reality and merely, abstract conceptualization, conviction or belief. It provides a sensibility towards the character and disposition that signifies absolute authenticity. Consequently, from the perspective of a familiarity with certainty, all things can be compared and adjudged for their foundational merit.

If we lack an essential precedent that epitomizes absolute surety, despite conviction concerning our position and however supported our standpoint may be by consensus, we can never decisively claim irrefutable, existential knowledge. Conversely, with the establishment of a benchmark that is secured upon our own direct experience of the essential condition of our singular existence, the tenor of every philosophical or religious proposition may be tried and contrasted for its ultimate significance. From one essential certainty, all other pronouncements and attestations concerning the nature of existence may be estimated for their merit.

But the recognition of the human, essential ipseity is of even more profound significance than the establishment of a qualitative standard of that which constitutes reality. Human, intrinsic significance resides within a converse condition to physicality. Therein, the essential connotation of everything is discernible. Thus, we become accustomed to the unique anomaly of our personal existence and thereby discover the imperative significance beyond the corporeal, of everyone and everything else.

Nevertheless, discernment of the intangible, essential dimension of things only inadequately addresses the human, essential malaise of self-circumscription. The subsequent estrangement from meaningful coexistence continues because we feel incidental through an underlying disorientation which, through self-interest, is antagonistic towards impartiality and probity.

However, to the degree that we permit supernal caritas to assure us of the immutable permanency of our existence, paradoxically, we relinquish our hold upon self-concern. Moreover, we begin to recognize the essential significance of other people and the intrinsic nature of phenomena, as our mentality becomes increasingly amenable towards a diametrically composed, essential existence. We recognize that the appearances of things are merely the superficial countenance while the quintessential alone exemplifies the significant. And we discover that the optimum perspective is contingent upon our mental and emotional condition.

In fact, the one certainty that we can rely on is that we persistently view existence erroneously and it is the ramifications of an essential falsity of perspective that requires reparation. We reposition the heart away from self-concern by making the psyche entirely vulnerable to restorative influence of supernal caritas whereby no dispositional penchant remains concealed. The accumulation of ages of misperception is resolved through the establishment of a gracious disposition that is without selfish incentive.

Resentments and regrets, base proclivities and avarice, are resolved through catharsis under a benign advocacy that reveals the authentic status of an existence which is beyond the self-circumscribed perspective. Subsequently, our viewpoint diametrically alters from self-concern to impartial magnanimity.

We gradually establish a new disposition that is not driven by self-gratification and we recognize existence from an essential perspective that is untarnished by self-concern. The petty sense-of-self is willingly abandoned when we recognize the obsolescence of a redundant mindset. Thereby, we find that we essentially occupy an incorporeal status wherein our authentic identification is utterly secure.

Furthermore, we are no longer preoccupied with calculated and argumentative speculation concerning existence, inflamed by erratic affection and partisan zeal. We exhibit the measured perspective that is established upon essential reality and not merely as we imagine or hope things might be. Consequently, without self-preoccupation, we avoid rancor and inevitably absolve one another of our transgressions because our viewpoint has become impartial and accordingly compassionate.

Thus, the human, fundamental malaise of self-circumscription is dissolved through an intimate magnanimity that is itself equitable and sympathetic. Through openhearted vulnerability, we inaugurate a process of reconciliation that corresponds with essential reality. The former, superficial perspective is recognized for its deficiency of meaningfulness, as purpose and value stimulate our determination to persevere and embrace the new human, paradigm.

The reorientation of the human disposition is crucial and without alternative because our familiar condition and approach towards existence is untenable. Inevitably, it will lead only to antagonism and dismay on an unprecedented scale particularly in the light of the rampant explosion in technology that makes our correspondences with one another increasingly indifferent and remote.

Through reorientation away from self-circumscription, we discover the essential condition of ourselves, others and phenomena, and we confirm the validity of our new viewpoint as the human, essential ipseity becomes increasingly evident as our authentic identification. We find that it no longer matters what happens to the petty sense-of-self because we no longer identify with it.

Similarly, before long, we discover the immanent condition wherein resides meaningfulness and purpose and thereby we confirm the authenticity of the direct, cognitive approach. But the constitution of the human psyche is transformed not through existential knowledge alone but by the direct and intimate experience of supernal caritas that resides within that same compass of immanence.

17. The Immanency of Supernal Amity

We supersede the dominant mindset of the segregated, petty sense-of-self through the realization that we cannot self-transform from a moribund mentality, but we must rely upon the extrinsic amity of supernal goodwill.

Through the anguish that arises from disparity with the graciousness that we directly and intimately experience within the heart, together with the persistent reproach of conscience, we find ourselves compelled to reexamine the circumstances of our restlessness. Thus, we convey our concerns and confide our disquietude and remorse to the immanency of supernal kindness.

Thereby, an implicit concurrence is instantly established, and we open the heart in earnest candor. Forthwith, we find ourselves beautifully restored by wisdom and we recognize that our inner tractability towards supernal caritas has commuted our distress into right-mindedness.

Those things that hinder our independence from a self-circumscribed, narrow perspective include deceptions that we recognize as such but rationalize as acceptable. We wish to retain aspects of fantasy because they are compelling but this makes a mockery of our endeavors and, accordingly, we only betray ourselves.

There is only one reality and it is that which we desire to discover. We cannot, in all sincerity, foster aspects of misconception and simultaneously render the heart vulnerable to a successive disposition because we delude ourselves through subterfuge. Artifice of this nature harms our progression because we cannot advance towards wholeness if we foster conceptual preference and duplicity. Thereby, we only work against our own best interest and, presently, we do not possess the leisure to dally.

The retention of unethical behaviors is similarly detrimental because we cannot selectively approach supernal caritas through openhearted sincerity. Openhearted sincerity includes neither contingency nor reservation because it is the entirety of our psyche that needs reorientation away from self-circumscription. To desire the disposal merely of characters and behaviors that are distasteful to us ignores the fundamental objective of dispositional remediation. Thus, the retention of acrimony, impropriety or dissolution reveals persistent, essential disorientation.

The entirety of the heart requires reestablishment. Our task is forthright and scrupulous candor towards the purgative and restorative influence of supernal caritas. Without artless simplicity we fail to accommodate the necessary corrective that transforms our demeanor. Without wholehearted concurrence the metamorphic transposition from self-circumscription to sovereign autonomy cannot be accomplished.

We recognize the immediate presence of supernal caritas, through direct experience. If it were remote and there was no such thing as immanent volume wherein all meaning resides, we would be unable to coincide with the exemplary nature through openhearted sincerity.

Similarly, if supernal caritas was nonexistent and merely illusory, then the metamorphic commutation of the heart from self-concern as a primary viewpoint, to the immediate recognition of the essential distinction of others, would be merely a chimerical concept.

But we describe these circumstances, not to pose a hypothetical scenario but because they reveal a greater spectrum to existence than merely the peripheral appearance and obvious condition of things. From the perspective of exclusive physicality, circumstances are bereft of content and attendant significance and an atrocious deception is thereby imposed, with disastrous consequences for humanity.

Of itself, this alone should be a compelling motivation for impartial, empirical research. But materialistic, Western philosophy contends that structure and composition is possible without connotation. Thus, organization is conjectured to self-originate which is an alien concept in human affairs but nonetheless reputed to exist in Natural circumstances even though it would require spontaneous magical instigation.

For example, through impartial observation and discernment we examine the humanly manufactured item and immediately recognize the intangible, conceptual origin that is represented by its completion. Similarly, we observe a Natural object in the same impartial manner and likewise we discern a formative intention. Thus, readily through direct observational engagement, the straightforward approach allows us to objectively contemplate two conditions and discover a qualitative similarity of causality.

Therefore, it is essential that we question the established doctrine and convention. It is entirely our own responsibility to independently weigh matters that are of vast, personal importance for ourselves and avoid the easy expedient of assuming an accustomed orthodoxy.

18. Metamorphic Transpiration

That things not only alter but improve is an article of faith, and the boldest of evolutionary conceptions. How far it be true were very hard to say; but I for one imagine that a pterodactyl flew no less well than does an albatross, and that Old Red Sandstone fishes swam as well and easily as the fishes of our own seas.

D'Arcy Wentworth Thompson (1860 - 1948) On Growth and Form (Chapter 12, page 873)

Organic complexity implies the existence of prevision because a future condition is foreseen to arise that cannot occur spontaneously. An organism possesses a compound, systematic order that is unlike the merely haphazard coincidence of different, characteristic deposits of the mineral kingdom. If we imagine that organization of any nature may emerge impulsively through the physical or chemical conditions of matter, we fail to grasp the basic cause-and-effect nature of those disciplines. Furthermore, if indifferent forces were alone responsible for organic life then all chemistry would have to be biochemistry because dead minerals do not incline towards automatic, organic organization.

Consequently, biological elaboration beyond a predictable chain of reactive circumstances is impossible because it would be without origin and therefore it would defy physical and chemical law. In other words, the repercussions of physical correspondence always equal a particular incentive and momentum and, consequently, with sufficient specialized knowledge, they are consistently predictable. Similarly, in chemistry the impetus resides within the qualitative attributes of the particular elements and their combinations but there is no ingenuity or resourcefulness present that is easily recognizable in biology.

The speculation that organic complexity may be derived from physical and chemical conditions is an entirely abstract notion that does not withstand even cursory empirical examination. Lifeless chain reactions cannot produce incommensurate developments but must always remain merely cause-and-effect. That is to say, chain reaction is incommensurate with biological organization.

The proportion missing from the lifeless analogy of living conditions is metamorphic transpiration which is of far greater complexity than merely the reactive response of forces. An inverse structure emerges which pursues an entirely different objective. Thus, the concentrated seed is comprehensively disparate both in form and function to the leaf or the flower and yet it remains qualitatively and essentially identical irrespective of its physical appearance. While, the plant follows a course of development that is both cyclical, progressive and purposeful, nothing like that is found within the disciplines of mechanics or chemistry. That is to say, physical interactions are accountable and measurable and similarly, chemical interactions remain predictably consistent. But neither specialization is applicable to Natural interpretation because they deal only with the inert properties of circumstances.

Direction that is beyond predictable reaction is found spectacularly in biological metamorphosis which sets it qualitatively apart from the mundane particulars of physics and chemistry. There is no determination towards complex construction in either of those other studies. But determination towards an entirely transposed appearance and objective is readily discernible in Nature.

It is through impartial observation and discernment concerning the phenomenon of metamorphosis that purpose is discerned. We recognize conditions that are conceived with intention and no physical force or chemical combination can consort to duplicate them because organic resourcefulness does not originate within the technical aspects of phenomena.

That is to say, resourcefulness is a qualitative, intangible capability that is peculiar to the activity of conceptualization. However, action and reaction, chains of circumstances and cause and effect are aimless and contrary to the objective that is everywhere discernible in the living world and epitomized by organic transformation. In other words, capricious, haphazard events do not conceive order.

If an advanced organism originated from a primitive life as is popularly surmised, that would constitute an effect without commensurate cause, which in terms of both physics and chemistry is nonsensical. The appeal of speculation and the human fascination with deduction as a means to discover the nature of things, are the direct result of an ignorance of immediate cognition. We imagine that rationale is our supreme cognitive asset but only in terms of hypothetical deliberation, can it seem perfectly reasonable that something should emanate from nothing However, in reality this kind of thinking merely reveals perceptive inadequacy.

Every organism must always fully function otherwise it would be untenable and disintegrate. The primordial creature must have been as integrated and organically faultless then as now or it would have been impractical. Evolution, as a concept of progressive development from elementary life towards sophistication, is predicated upon the assumption of impulsive enhancement for which there is no apparent impetus because physical conditions and innate forces that are non-creative.

These things are not difficult to discern through immediate cognition because the direct approach occurs without preemptive bias. However, rationale, unlike the precision of mathematics, is imprecise because logic is not mathematics but it is strongly influenced by predilections. Inevitably, our support of a certain position will be persuaded by preference because, without direct cognition, we cannot impartially observe and discover the intrinsic condition of things but we must evaluate and surmise indirectly concerning them, which involves the preferential selection of suitable ideas.

19. Intangible Significance

Through a determined denial of significance to anything but the material status of things, we have managed to contrive a philosophical approach to life that is counter to reality. But we know from conventional experience that there is compelling and impressive evidence for the existence of an intangible volume to phenomena. Although physically elusive, the quality of something, for example, while different from the appearance, yet remains as meaningful as the physical condition. If we envisage existence without quality or intrinsic distinction we quickly discover that bereft of intangible value, our interpretation of life appears monochrome.

The quality of something is only discovered experientially. Quantification cannot depict value but merely provides a scale of calibration derived from the distantly related physical circumstances. For example, we may inquire as to the identification of a primary color such as red. The quality of red must be experienced in order to be known and it is all but impossible to describe to a blind person without resort to analogy and metaphor the disposition of a color. But through figuration we can then describe how warm a particular red may be on a scale of one to ten, one perhaps being the coldest. But number one does not describe the quality of the color itself, it merely offers a convenient measure whereby we avoid metaphoric analogy.

Value is not represented physically but exists as the qualitative contingency of the authentic identity that is the intrinsic nature. Pursued further, we recognize that all things possess an intangible significance wherein the meaningfulness of the phenomenon resides. Thus, we discover that there exists an entirely, physically inaccessible volume of implicit implication that cannot be represented in technical terms.

Unfortunately, we have grown accustomed to an overemphasis upon physically explicit circumstances at the expense of intrinsic significance, and we imagine that the extraneous countenance is the extent of the identification of phenomena. Consequently, scientific inquiry is inevitably prejudiced because it requires materially substantial data and it cannot approve incorporeal value or recognize imperative importance. That is to say, empirical research implies the necessity of proof. But without material representation proof is impossible. Thus, a methodology that excludes information because it is intrinsically unable to manage it by virtue of its exclusivity, will fail to achieve conclusive findings if the nature of the evidence extends beyond the limited parameters of the approach.

Inversely, if we accept that the materially exclusive inquiry solely concedes those properties of phenomena that are without qualitative dimension, we must deduce that existence is essentially sterile. We conclude that life is merely an automated progression or the consequence of an accidental amalgamation of countless physical assets that exploded into structure and organization. We arrive at this austere conclusion because, through abstract intellection, we have managed to rob life of all essential substance by concentrating exclusively upon the material status of things. Compounded by the conviction that life is impulsively born of lifeless circumstances, the materialist disdainfully derides those whose experiences lead to an opposite conclusion. But the conceit of this brand of atheism is that it is really a belief system alike to any other and no more insightful than any other dogma.

Through immediate cognition, the fallacy of slanted and oblique thinking becomes obvious because we engage circumstances directly without the impediment of philosophy, hypothesis or abstract rationale. Thereby, we meet a situation straightforwardly and avoiding the interference of foreknowledge, we discover things in their elemental condition. Thus, we are able to ascertain the full dimensionality of phenomena because we engage them not askance as we think or imagine them to be but originally, as if for the first time.

When we directly determine the intrinsic condition of something or of another person, we access the immanent volume of existence wherein the essential of things resides. This is not a place but it is the overlooked continuum that extends beyond the merely, hard physical condition. Thus, from the perspective of intrinsic infinity, the concept of an isolated, corporeal status that we assume comprises the entirety of existence, appears impoverished and superficial.

Recognition of the essential significance of others, the elemental particularity of a mineral or of a color and the discovery of the archetypal origin of organic diversity, reveals the meaningful dimensionality of existence, which is also reality. The direct experience of consequential volume presents the physically elusive magnitude and the inherent proportion of things to us. Furthermore, immediate engagement and the discovery of essential significance favorably alter the human disposition because we move away from superficiality and develop a sensibility for the profoundness of existence that is the beginning of wisdom.

20. Conclusion

The dogmas of a particular body are accepted and embraced by those people who desire admittance into that society. The reception of a member is contingent upon the adoption of the tenets of that community and of acquiescence to the authority of the company. Thus, the individual relinquishes self-determination and conforms to an existing architecture that imposes its governance over the membership.

Similarly, there is nothing mysterious or inexplicable except through human, cognitive inhibition. We are limited by a certain myopia that prevents us from discovering the authentic condition of things. A fixation with the tangible representation of phenomena causes us to assume that physicality is the full extent of existence. However, through the practice of immediate cognition, the human, essential ipseity discovers the intrinsic nature and intangible volume of things wherein lie the meaning and determination.

Thus, we no longer require the explanation and clarification of an elite scholarship nor do not heed the authority of a religious or philosophical elite. We find that no one possesses a monopoly of knowledge that disregards our own direct engagement of circumstances and we refuse to acquiesce to anything that contradicts our own explicit apprehension.

Inherent in the fabric of existence resides the entirety of human emancipation. Where it is complicated and concealed from sincere and straightforward inquiry by the dogma of a particular organization, we find not enlightenment but human fabrication.

Thus, we find the answers to the dilemmas of human existence within those circumstances that immediately pertain to our particular quandary but not in contrived systems and structures of human elaboration. It is because many religious and philosophical perspectives are frequently, humanly devised and embellished that they are antagonistic to one another and share little common ground.

Through immediate cognition, we engage circumstances originally and we recognize the intangible volume that is disregarded by materialistic, Western philosophy. The overlooked intrinsic significance of things such as the qualitative temper of a particular color or the inherent distinction and essential aspect of a mineral is found to exemplify the authentic appellation. Wherever we find a particular color, we identify it by its intrinsic characteristics which never change because the qualitative significance is the authentic nomen.

Similarly, we listen to the calls of different birds and thereby we discover the qualitative distinction that expresses the same bid principle according to a particular, characteristic demeanor and temperament that, once recognized, is similarly found to be its authentic identification. The cry epitomizes the identity of the creature which is further expressed in its appearance and behavior.

Comparing the particular expressions of creatures and the different ways in which the commonalities that they share are expressed, we recognize that an intangible idiosyncratic distinctiveness belies the physical properties. We find that appearance is dominated by the qualitative demeanor of the creature. Additionally, we discover that a reciprocal interaction occurs between the particular form and the temperament of the animal. This is an aspect of the greater ecology towards which the organism qualitatively responds, and it thereby adjusts in form through alteration in its dispositional expression.

We learn the nature of existence not from a popular account or through the adoption of an approved philosophy but directly, for ourselves. Subsequently, we discover the way that things exist in reality and we align our volition and sentiment accordingly. We refuse to be deceived by an elite authority that purports to possess superior information to our own because we have engaged circumstances directly and we recognize the tone of authenticity.

Human autonomy lies in the recognition of things as they exist in their entirety, coupled with a concomitant moral standing that is established within the human heart by supernal caritas and through our own guileless and straightforward willingness.

95

UNDER THE AEGIS OF IMMANENT CARITAS
The Reorientation of the Human, Disparate Self-circumscribed Mentality

THE DECEPTION OF MATERIALISTIC WESTERN PHILOSOPHY
An Exploration of the Physically Elusive Volume of Existence

THE OBSOLETE SELF
Individual Uniqueness and Significance beyond Egocentrism

HUMAN SOVEREIGN AUTONOMY
The Discovery of the Human Ipseity and its Establishment as the Essential Authority of the Human Constitution

THE TRANSFORMATION OF THE SOUL
From Self-centeredness to Sovereign Autonomy

THE IMPLICATION OF HUMAN, INCORPOREAL EXISTENCE
The Overlooked Significance of the Intangible and Qualitative Dimension of Existence

IMMEDIATE EXPERIENTIAL COGNITION
The Inherent Human Capacity of Immediate Engagement

KNOWLEDGE THROUGH DIRECT COGNITION
The Human Conscious Individuality and Immediately Experienced Reality

www.ingramcontent.com/pod-product-compliance
Lightning Source LLC
Chambersburg PA
CBHW060551100426

42742CB00013B/2517